THE BLAME GAME IS OVER
Becoming a Better You

THE BLAME GAME IS OVER
Becoming a Better You

LAQUETIA YVONNE MERCER

Glimpse of Glory
CHRISTIAN BOOK PUBLISHING

TABLE OF CONTENTS

ACKNOWLEDGEMENTS

I would like to thank the loves of my life, my children, Kormaine Marquis Woods, Jermiah Yvonne Brown, and Jermaine Lamon Brown, Jr., for being supportive and for loving me and encouraging me when I did not love myself. I am honored that God chose me to be your mother, my children.

I would like to thank my grannys, MacKenzie Elise Woods and Kormaine Marquis Woods, Jr., and their mother, Mharlena Ayers. I am forever thankful and grateful for each of you.

To my mom, Yvonne Terrell Williams, and my dad, Bradley Clarke Mercer, Jr., I want to thank you both from the bottom of my heart. There would be no me without both of you.

To my sisters, Yalandas Faye Mercer and Eboni Lynn Streeter, my brother, Leonard Streeter, Jr., and my niece, Shuntae LaFaye Mercer, I love you all to the moon and back. Eboni, thank you for capturing beautiful pictures of me for my book cover! To our bestie, Tyesha Latrelle Huggins, thank you. Love you.

To my brothers, Mario Lamont Forbes of Detroit Michigan, and Stephon Hill of Birmingham, Alabama, I love you both.

I would like to thank my mother's sister, the late Glenda Faye Terrell Turner (auntie Glenda) and her brothers, William Russell Terrell, Jr. (uncle Coochie), Douglas Terrell (uncle Doug), Dewayne Terrell (uncle Pap), and the late Joe Nathan Terrell (uncle Joe), and Gary Norris (uncle Gary) for being a part of my life. I love each of you. And to my dad's sisters, Shelia Mercer (auntie Sheila), Kimberlee Mercer (auntie Kim), and Evangeline Doby (auntie Van) and his brothers, Donald Earl Mercer (uncle Donald Earl), Gilbert Mercer (uncle Gilbert), and Benjamin Mercer (uncle Ben). I thank each of you for being a part of my life, too, and I love you all. I will be forever grateful for all of my aunties, uncles, and the rest of my family.

I would like to thank my two ex-husbands, Korey Dewayne Woods and Jermaine Lamon Brown, and my first love, Roviar Finch, for the many lessons and blessings.

I would like to thank Pastor CJ and First Lady Kenisha Anderson of Life Changing Worship Center in Birmingham, Alabama. I appreciate you both for pushing me and supporting me.

I would like to thank Pastor Harold W. Bass of Olivet Monumental Baptist Church in Birmingham, Alabama. I answered the call upon my life under your leadership on October 24, 2012. You are very instrumental in my Christian walk.

I would like to thank the late Reverend Hobdy Moorer, Jr., a former Pastor of 6th Street Peace Baptist Church in Birmingham, Alabama. My spiritual foundation begin under your leadership when I was a little girl.

I would like to thank Yolanda Marshall Nickerson for being who God created her to be. Thank you for helping me, encouraging me, and coaching me along the way. Thank you for allowing God to use you to make my dream and His plan come true.

In loving memory of
my grandparents, Mamie Lee Brown Terrell, William Russell
Terrell, Sr., Susie Mae Mercer, Bradley Clarke Mercer, Sr., and
my aunt, Glenda Faye Terrell Turner, and my uncle Joe Nathan
Terrell. They all played major roles in my life. Love and kisses
to Heaven to each of you.

"And we know that in all things God works for the good of those who love him, who have been called according to his purpose."
Romans 8:28 NIV

INTRODUCTION

God is in control. He also gives us a certain amount of control over our lives. God gives us free will. He does not hold us down and choke us into allowing Him in our lives. No matter what decisions we make, He still loves us anyway. God's love is unconditional. His love is also eternal. God did not create us to live an unhappy, complicated, and stressful life. His desire is for us to live an abundant, peaceful, happy life. It is time to take full responsibility for your life and let the blame game be over.

The Merriam-Webster Dictionary defines blame as "to place responsibility for." Blaming has existed since the beginning of time. In Genesis 2:15-17 NLT, "The Lord God placed the man in the Garden of Eden to tend and watch over it. But the Lord God warned him, "You may freely eat the fruit of every tree in the garden—except the tree of

knowledge of good and evil. If you eat its fruit, you are sure to die." Genesis 3:11-13 NLT says, "Who told you that you were naked?" the Lord God asked." Have you eaten from the tree whose fruit I commanded you not to eat?" The man replied, *"It was the woman you gave me who gave me the fruit, and I ate it."* Then the Lord God asked the woman, "What have you done?" *"The serpent deceived me,"* she replied. *"That's why I ate it."* The Bible shows us how Adam blamed Eve in Genesis 3:12 and how Eve blames the serpent in Genesis 3:13.

Are you a person that will lie and blame others for something you do wrong or are you the one who is often lied on and blamed for something others do wrong? Did you know that the trait of lying and blaming others for something you do wrong is very dangerous, and it can easily cause you to destroy the lives of others emotionally, mentally, socially, financially, and even spiritually? You may have heard people say "Right is right and wrong is wrong." It is always right to accept responsibility for your actions and it is always wrong to blame others to deflect punishment or consequences away from yourself when you do something wrong.

Many of us learned as children how to tell lies and blame others to deflect punishment or consequences away from ourselves when we did something wrong. Even though we were guilty, we chose to lie about that something to keep from facing the consequences of our actions. If you did not experience this as a child, you probably know someone else who did. When we adopt this kind of behavior as a child, it can easily spill over into our adulthood and we will find ourselves carrying it out throughout our lives unless we make a conscious decision to change our ways.

You see, some of us will go through life blaming someone else for something that we should hold ourselves accountable for. We will blame God for the negative things we encounter in life when we actually caused those things to happen to us. We will blame our parents for the way we were raised when we actually rebelled against their leadership and failed to heed their instructions. We will blame our job because we do not like it and are not making enough money when we actually neglect to do what is required of us as an employee. We will blame our friends for what they do or don't do for us when that friend has shown themselves to be no good for us. We will blame our children for being disobedient when we are not leading by example. We will blame our spouse, partner, boyfriend, or girlfriend for the problems in our relationship when we are the one causing the problems. The person you are married to or in a relationship with or the one you are no longer with was your decision. They showed you who they were in the beginning of

14

the relationship, but you still moved forward with them. Maya Angelou said, "When someone shows you who they are, believe them the first time." Some people will make you think they are "down to earth" and they will be your "ride or die," as some of us might say, but they are the total opposite. Believe what they show you. Some people do not want to be better or change their ways.

I want you to really understand how important it is to blame yourself for the decisions you make in life, and not anyone else. We can no longer shift the blame when we should blame ourselves for our own decisions. It is time for us to become self-aware and take responsibility for our lives. It is time for us to be better and do better, individually.

Sometimes you have to ask yourself some of the toughest questions, just like I found myself having to do. Ask yourself these questions: What are my toxic behaviors? Am I overeating, overspending, gossiping, doing drugs, consuming too much alcohol, fornicating, engaging in pornography, lying, cheating, always feeling the need to be in a relationship, continuing to connect with negative-minded people, etc.? Am I trying to fill a void within me that could be drawing me to toxic people and causing me to carry out certain behaviors in my life? Why do I keep going from man to man or woman to woman? Could it be because I do not want to be alone? Why do I allow certain people or things in my life on a daily basis? Are they toxic? Are they extremely negative? Do they blame everyone else for their problems? Pay attention to what they are saying because a person will show their true self very early, especially in a relationship that is less likely to last. Listen to how they explain what they have been through and how it is affecting them now. Are they still upset for something that happened 10, 20, 30 or 40 years ago? At some point, they have to decide to deal with that and move on. There is most definitely nothing you can do about it, but you can pray for that person and let God work on them. Each of us has to allow God to work on us. He can heal us, deliver us, and set us free from anything that hinders us from moving forward.

Anytime we find ourselves repeating negative life cycles, we have to get to the root of the problem and see if that is what is causing us to behave a certain way. After we do that, then we can be healed emotionally and mentally, have peace, and move forward in our lives. Now I must say that if you are dealing with something that you absolutely had no control over, such as rape, abuse, death, illness, or something else traumatic from your childhood, you could not control what happened to you, but you can control your reaction. I encourage you to get some help as soon as possible and make a decision to forgive the person or people who may have violated you in some kind of way. Forgive others and then forgive yourself. Do not ever hesitate to pray either. God will not only hear your prayers, He will answer every single one of them, and He will help you, too.

As you read this book, you will learn how to become a better you. Sometimes you can be hindered by your own self. So, from this moment, do away with blaming others for anything that pertains to you and just aim high at becoming the best version of yourself so that you can get the best out of life, in every area of your life. At the end of each chapter, you will find a section called Quetia's Nuggets, which are messages that I encourage you to meditate on and think about how they may relate to you now or in your past. There is also a journal in the back of the book. You may write notes to yourself and make sure you add the date of your notes. Also, you can write down your thoughts and answer the journal questions. This will allow you to revisit and re-read this book and reflect upon your thoughts and answers at a later time so that you can evaluate your progression.

THE BLAME GAME IS OVER

I am not sharing my story to be judged or persecuted. I am sharing my story so that God can get the Glory. My story is, in essence, God's story, because He had a plan and purpose for everything that I have gone through. I am reminded of what His Word says in 2 Corinthians 12:9 NIV: "My grace is sufficient for you, for my power is made perfect in weakness." His grace saved me from myself and some of the decisions I made that I am not proud of, that I had to face consequences for. His grace pulled me out of some of the deepest pits I found myself in. God is faithful and He has never lied to me nor has He ever left or forsaken me.

When I became an adult, I found myself playing the blame game. I blamed my grandparents for dying and leaving me. I blamed others for certain things, including the relationships and marriages that I chose to be in. I had been running from myself and blaming others for some of the decisions I made, that did not turn out the way that I wanted them to. I have not always owned my part for some of the things that I have done. I have had seven miscarriages and three abortions. I have had several failed relationships, two divorces, and a called-off engagement. After dealing with so many losses, from grieving the death of loved ones to having those miscarriages and abortions to the failed relationships and divorces, I wondered how I would even come back from all of it.

My previous failed relationships and marriages stemmed from me making rash, quick decisions, over and over again. I was not fully taking time to really get to know the men that I dated prior to really giving myself away to them. I had sex before marriage several times and, if the truth be told, if the sex was good, my judgment became cloudy and I was not focused on how I would end up feeling after the "thrill was gone." As a result of this, I ended up crying and hurting because none of the relationships lasted. Sadly, they all ended. I learned that it was not love after all.

I have also learned over the years what it really means to love someone and not lust after them. Lusting after someone can lead to only having sex with them, and sex before marriage does not fulfill your need to love and be loved by someone. Some men and women do not even want to commit to a relationship nor will they consider marriage, so don't let anyone tell you that you need to test the car before driving it. This is what some of us might say when we refer to having sex with someone before marriage. Now if you have only been with one person who is now your husband or wife and you all took the time to date and really got to know one another fully, have already fallen in love, and had sex, then eventually you will think each other is the greatest and the best because you have no one to compare to. That is God's design. It is a beautiful thing. The beauty of having sex in a marriage is more fulfilling than having it with someone that you are not married to.

I remember the times I used sex as a Band-Aid to cover up my hurt, pain, and problems. I wanted that good, temporary feeling of having sex, all while I was hurting on the inside. I was creating soul ties with the men that I slept with outside of marriage. I found myself carrying the men that I had sex with in my spirit. I was seeking unconditional love from earthly men and not realizing that God could offer me what I needed the entire time. It was not until later that I learned how to wait on God's timing for everything that pertains to me, including marriage. I now realize that sex is only meant for a husband and wife. That is the order of God.

Speaking of order, I can honestly say that I was out of order in those seasons of my life. I literally felt like I was a mess. But God has turned my "mess into a message." It is only by His grace that I have a clear, sound, and renewed mind today. With this clear, sound, and renewed mind, I realize that God never meant for any of us to have to endure such pain. His plan for each of us is for good. You see, I was giving away the most precious thing that I have, just like giving a child candy without a second thought. I was giving my mind, body, and spirit to men that did not even think enough to marry me, although later I married twice.

There were times in my previous marriage where I experienced waking up with heartaches, due to certain things that happened. There were times I did not want to even get out of bed. Sometimes, when our heart is broken, our life is, too. I felt this way. You may currently feel this way. There were times that I could not see the beauty in anything. I could not even think of anything inspirational and, to be honest, I did not even want to. I held so many things in for so long, not allowing myself to feel the fullness of anything. I had been one big wall, desiring to help free others when I had not been freed myself. I guarded myself not only from pain, but from genuine joy, as well. Ever since my grandmother passed away on December 25, 2001, I struggled with living. I felt like I was dealing with a double dose of pain—the pain from my grandmother's death and the pain from two divorces.

During my darkest days, I had to continuously pray to God for strength as well as for Him to remove the hurt from my heart. I began to see that everything that I was holding onto in my previous marriage was not hurting anyone but me. I literally

21

felt like I was in bondage. I was in prison mentally, physically, emotionally, spiritually, and financially. There were times I did not feel like I was being the best version of me.

I learned that some of what I had experienced in my previous marriage really distracted me from having those much-needed conversations with God. And, there were times I did not have any real peace or joy. I am reminded of what John 10:10 KJV says: "The thief cometh not, but for to steal, and to kill, and to destroy: God says I am come that they might have life, and that they might have it more abundantly." I felt like the devil had stolen my peace and my joy.

I consistently found myself rehearsing the negative things that happened over and over in my mind. It was not until I had to face myself and realize that after all I endured, I was the one who made the decisions to do what I did in the first place. I chose to marry and I chose to divorce. Divorce hurts, but divorce did not free me. I had to allow God to free me and heal me. I literally had to be honest with myself and God about the mess I created and some of the life-changing decisions I made. I did not ask God about some of the decisions I made, including marriage. I felt like I dismissed some of the red flags that He showed me. For me, I felt like my judgment was clouded by other things: sex before marriage, loneliness, and not being emotionally and mentally healed for any kind of relationship, let alone marriage. You see, I accepted and allowed people in my life that were there for different reasons. I tried to make lifetime people out of seasonal people.

When it was all said and done, I had to make a decision to be better and do better. I had to want to be better for me and my children. I had to blame myself and not others for my decisions, because rehearsing the same blame song had gotten old. I had to literally step back and take a good look in the mirror and take

22

full responsibility for my life. That was the start of my healing process. Before I decided to look in the mirror and really deal with myself, I was stuck mentally, physically, emotionally, spiritually, and financially. And I felt like I was imprisoned in my mind, and I was the one who did it to myself. It was 2007 when I put myself in prison in my mind by allowing myself to stoop to someone else's level. I learned that you can fight back, and you can fuss and cuss in a relationship or a marriage, but over a period of time you will lose yourself. I can honestly say today, just as I shared before, I am free. On January 7, 2020, I made a mental decision to let go of the things that I was holding on to in my second marriage. It took my heart to say, "No more." It took my pain to push me. It took both prayer and forgiveness. It took the strength of God. It took my willingness to follow God's leading. I decided that I want to finally live and not just exist, and to help others through my story, my testimony, and the message that is shared in this book.

CHAPTER ONE
SELF-EVALUATION

"Thus saith the Lord of hosts; consider your ways."
Haggai 1:7 KJV

"Without proper self-evaluation, failure is inevitable."
-John Wooden

The Merriam-Webster Dictionary defines "self-evaluation" as "one self or one's actions, performance or etc."

It is necessary to "consider your ways," all of your ways, and do a self-evaluation. I mean a true, deep self-evaluation. Having to take a hard look at yourself may not be an easy thing to do, but it is the right thing to do. I remember having to look in the mirror and ask myself what was my part in every situation I encountered. I encourage you to do the same. No matter if you are hurting right now. No matter if you are down right now. No matter if you are in the middle of a trial right now. No matter what, a self-evaluation is needed for change as well as growth in every area of your life.

When you decide to do a self-evaluation, and I encourage you to do it soon enough, you will learn things that you may or may not have known about yourself, whether it be good or bad. By the time you are done evaluating yourself, you will know just how much you need God to help you from the inside out, heal you from the inside out, and "make you over" from the inside out. Each of us has flaws, shortcomings, and problems that we cannot fix on our own. We need the One who created us to help us on our journey in life.

God knows your need for change, so never be afraid to let Him know how much you need Him. He knows that you need His help. He wants to change you so that you can be your best self, so get ready for a change of heart, a change of mind, a change for Him! Your change may not come immediately, but it will come. Forgiving and being forgiven is what He wants for you. Anger, bitterness, hurt, jealousy, envy or strife is what He wants to rid you of. He wants to remove the Band-Aids of hurt. He wants to remove the cushions of sin. He wants to cleanse and heal you for real.

QUETIA'S NUGGETS

❖ Consider all of your ways, not just some of them. When you do so, you will see clearly the areas of change that are needed in your life.

❖ Perform a self-assessment daily. Make sure you check your motives. Ask yourself why you do what you do or don't do. This can and will keep you on track.

❖ No matter how perfect you think you may be, there will always be areas of your life that you need to work on. Remember that you are not perfect. None of us are. If you were perfect, you would not need Jesus. Ask God to help you and clean your heart. Never ever think that you can make it without Him.

❖ Reflect upon your life. Strive to be better and do better.

❖ Be sure to connect with positive-minded people. Evaluate your friendships and your relationships. Know what someone truly is in a friendship or a relationship and not what you want them to be. What you want and what they are could be regions apart. Be honest with yourself.

❖ One of my problems is that I expect people to care like I care and love like I love. It is my own expectations that often hurt me. That may be the same for you, too. You must learn how to "Let go and let God," as some of us often say.

CHAPTER TWO
ADMIT AND CONFESS

"Confess your faults one to another and pray one for another, that ye may be healed. The effectual fervent prayer of a righteous man availeth much."
James 5:16 KJV

"It takes guts and humility to admit mistakes. Admitting we're wrong is courage, not weakness."
-Roy T. Bennett

"Confess you were wrong yesterday; it will show you are wise today.
-Proverb

The Merriam-Webster Dictionary defines admit as "to concede as true or valid," and it defines "confess" as "to tell or make known something, such as something wrong or damaging to oneself."

For some people, it is easy for them to admit and confess their faults, while others it is hard. They would rather blame others. If you are this kind of person, I want you to understand that it does not matter who or what you are blaming, self-awareness, admitting and confessing your own faults is the first step to becoming free in your mind, spirit, and soul. Don't allow the devil to rob you of living a great life by making you feel like admitting and confessing your faults is a bad thing. It is a good thing to own your part in any given situation.

You cannot go through life blaming others for something you did. The decisions you make to do this or that are yours and yours alone. I want you to understand that God gives you free will. But you have to remember that the decisions you make outside of His will are your own. That is why it is important to own what you have done and allowed in your life. It is also important to know that there are consequences for your actions. There is just absolutely no way to escape consequences. None of us are exempt from facing consequences for our actions.

I want to encourage you to take a moment to stand up and look in the mirror and admit and confess your faults as well as your bad habits, and then ask God to forgive you and help you start making better decisions in every area of your life. Listen to Him because we as humans sometimes have the wrong motives as to why we are making a particular decision at a certain time, instead of waiting on God to lead us.

<u>Quetia's Nuggets</u>

❖ Confess your faults and bad habits, even if it hurts you to do so.

❖ It is never okay to blame others. Quit pointing the finger at others when you should be pointing the finger at yourself.

❖ It is neither wrong nor a bad thing to admit to doing something wrong, especially when you are moving in the right direction in your life. Just pause for a moment and then say, "I did it and I was wrong for doing it."

❖ Sometimes your own decisions can often get in your way and cause an adverse effect in your life.

❖ You have to stop rehearsing the same negative things over and over again. When you do so, you give power to whatever it might be.

❖ Free your mind, spirit, and soul. Don't allow the devil to rob you of your freedom.

❖ Strive to make better decisions daily.

❖ Don't allow past situations or circumstances cause you to make bad decisions because you will have to be the one to face the consequences.

❖ Make a list of the things you would like for God to rid you from.

CHAPTER THREE
REPENT

2 Chronicles 7:14 KJV
"If my people which are called by my name shall humble themselves and pray and seek my face and turn from their wicked ways; then will I hear from heaven and will forgive their sin and will heal their land."
2 Chronicles 7:14 KJV

"No one can begin a new life, unless he repent of the old."
-Saint Augustine

The Merriam-Webster Dictionary defines "repent" as "to run from sin and dedicate oneself to the amendment of one's life."

I have learned that it is not only a good thing to repent to God daily, it is necessary for your spiritual growth. It is necessary to living a better life. You cannot expect to live your best life and receive an abundance of blessings from God when you continue sinning.

God sees every sin that you have committed, so you cannot blame someone else for your sinful actions either. I understand that some things can be generational curses as we all deal with some form of generational curse in our bloodline. But the key is that when God reveals whatever that generational curse is in your family, it is up to you to break it when it hits your life. Just because your mother or father or grandmother or grandfather lived a sinful life where they did all manners of things, it does not mean that you, too, have to live a sinful life. With God's help and your desire to break a generational curse of sin, it can be broken and you can become free. The Word of God tells us in Romans 3:23 KJV, "For all have sinned and come short of the glory of God," but your ultimate goal should be to not live a life of sin.

You have to come to a place in your life where you are willing and ready to repent and turn from whatever you are doing that is not pleasing unto God. Acts 3:19 NLT says, "Now repent of your sins and turn to God, so that your sins may be wiped away." It could be a toxic relationship where you are fornicating or drugs or lying or drunkenness, or something else. God will wipe it away. Give Him room to work in your life and grant you with one blessing after the next. That curse does not have to continue traveling from one generation to the next. The generational curse can stop with you.

I want to encourage you to declare with your mouth right now, "The generational curse of sin stops with me. No more living a sinful life that is not pleasing unto God." Whatever that sin is, declare, "No more." When you say it, mean it, and be sure you are ready to completely turn from it. And, remember that the Word of God tells us that "faith without works is dead" (Read James 2:26 KJV). That means even when you say it, you have to ensure that you do what is needed to stay away from it, even disconnecting from people who can entice you to do something that is not right. Make every effort to reject sin whenever you are tempted to engage in it. And always know that "You can do all things through Christ who strengthens you" (Philippians 4:13 KJV).

QUETIA'S NUGGETS

❖ Repent daily. Now repent of your sins and turn to God, so that your sins may be wiped away. (Acts 3:19 NLT)

❖ Don't make excuses to sin. It is wrong.

❖ Don't allow your emotions to influence you to yield to sin. Maintain self-control.

❖ You have a choice to sin or not. Make the choice to flee from sin.

❖ God wants you to live your best life.

❖ Disconnect from negative-minded people as well as those who entice you to do things that are wrong.

❖ Ask God to strengthen you.

❖ Make every effort to live a life that is pleasing unto God.

❖ As you strive to do well, you will find it easier to do well.

❖ Never refuse to get help.

❖ Surrender to God. Let Him know that you need His help. Remember, He has given His Angels charge over you, to keep you in all of your ways. (Read Psalm 91 KJV).

CHAPTER FOUR
FORGIVE YOURSELF AND OTHERS

"For if ye forgive men their trespasses, your heavenly Father will also forgive you. But if ye forgive not men their trespasses, neither will your Father forgive your trespasses."
Matthew 6:14-15 KJV

"To forgive is to set a prisoner free and discover that the prisoner was you."
-Lewis. R. Smedes

"Forgive others, not because they deserve it, but because you deserve peace."
-Jonathan Lockwood Huie

The Merriam-Webster Dictionary defines "forgiveness" as "the act of forgiving."

It is so very important to forgive yourself and others. Learning to forgive is a decision you must make. It is totally up to you to forgive yourself, and others who may wrong you. You may never get an apology, explanation, or acknowledgment from the person or people who may have wronged you. You just have to make up in your mind that you want to live a happy, fulfilled life, and you can only experience that kind of life when you truly forgive. Although some situations you encounter in life can make it seem hard to forgive, I can assure you that, once you learn to forgive, you will find that it will become much easier to experience freedom and peace in your mind, spirit, and soul. You will begin to blossom after you forgive that person or people you may have not forgiven. When you forgive others, it is really for you. It is like weights are literally lifted from your shoulders, as well as your heart.

Forgiveness is an act of obedience to God. It places you in a position to be forgiven by Him. When you refuse to forgive, you limit yourself from receiving blessings from God. You limit yourself from receiving help from others. You limit your ability to soar in life. You can even cause dysfunction in every area of your life. You can easily become mentally, emotionally, and spiritually stagnant. Some people have become physically sick just because they refused to forgive someone else. When you harbor unforgiveness in your heart, you literally open the door for the devil to come into your life and cause torment and unnecessary stress.

I want you to understand that God does not want that for your life. He wants you to experience His joy and peace. He wants you to be "kind one to another, tender hearted, forgiving one another, even as God for Christ's sake hath forgiven you" (Ephesians 4:32 KJV). Forgiveness does not always require that you forget what happened or minimize the wrong that you experienced, it just means that you simply need to let go of a matter for your own well-being.

QUETIA'S NUGGETS

❖ You must decide to forgive. Make a decision to forgive so that you can move forward. When you forgive, you will learn that it was the best thing you could have done.

❖ If you cannot forgive yourself, you may have a hard time forgiving others. When you don't forgive yourself first, you will easily allow yourself to become stuck mentally, emotionally, and even spiritually.

❖ When you do not repent and forgive, you put yourself into prison in your mind.

❖ Learn to release and give to God whatever has caused you to become offended.

❖ Vengeance is God's, not yours.

❖ Your decisions, actions, and reactions are yours alone.

❖ Forgiveness brings natural and spiritual blessings into your life.

❖ Some people refuse to forgive because of power. They will hinder forgiveness to maintain a sort of power over the offender. They will continue blaming and guilt tripping you until they can no longer do it. Don't allow that to be you.

FORGIVE

- ❖ **"F"** is for Free. Free yourself from holding someone else hostage in your mind. When you do not forgive, you will constantly think of that person or people who you refuse to forgive because you are reliving and rehearsing the offense over and over in your mind.

- ❖ **"O"** is for Obedience to God's Word. Matthew 6:14-15 KJV says, "For if ye forgive men their trespasses, your heavenly Father will also forgive you: But if ye forgive not men their trespasses; neither will your Father forgive your trespasses."

- ❖ **"R"** is for Repent. 2 Chronicles 7:14 KJV says, "If my people which are called by my name, shall humble themselves, and pray, and seek my face, and turn from their wicked ways: then will I hear from heaven, and will forgive their sin, and will heal their land."

- ❖ **"G"** is for Grace. Ephesians 2:8 KJV says, "For by grace are ye saved through faith; and that not of yourselves: it is the gift of God."

- ❖ **"I"** is for Instruction. 2 Timothy 3:16 KJV says, "All Scripture is given by inspiration of God, and is profitable for doctrine, for reproof, for correction, for instruction in righteousness."

- ❖ **"V"** is for Vengeance. Romans 12:19 KJV says, "Dearly beloved, avenge not yourselves, but rather give place unto wrath: for it is written, vengeance is mine: I will repay, saith the Lord."

- ❖ **"E"** is for Everlasting. John 3:16 KJV says, "For God so loved the world, that he gave his only begotten Son, that whosoever believeth in him should not perish, but have everlasting life."

CHAPTER FIVE
BE HEALED

"When Jesus saw him lie, and knew that he had been now a long time in that case, he saith unto him, Wilt thou be made whole?"
John 5:6 KJV

"Healing does not mean the damage never existed. It means the damage no longer controls our lives."
-Unknown

The Merriam-Webster Dictionary defines "healing" as "to make free from injury or disease: to make sound or whole, to make well again: to restore to health."

Becoming whole in every area of your life is essential in becoming a better you. When you are healed in every area of your life, you can easily blossom, just like a flower. People will see you glowing and know that God has made you whole. They will be drawn to you.

The emotional, mental, and spiritual healing process is the same and as equally important as physical. During the physical process of healing, some days are not going to feel so good. Some days will hurt more than other days, but one must expect a great outcome while going through the process of healing. You will feel much better when you do so.

True healing begins with you. You have to be honest with yourself concerning your need for healing. If you are sick in your body, when you go to the doctor, he or she wants to know what is going on with you. They are going to ask questions about what is hurting you, and if you are experiencing pain, they might ask what your level of pain is on a scale of 1 to10. In order for them to treat the problem and provide a prescription that will manifest healing, your honesty will be needed. So, the very first step is acknowledging that there is a problem, an injury, or a hurt, and then you can move in the direction of doing what is needed to secure your healing.

Just like you can experience a physical sickness, you can go through things in your friendships, relationships, etc. that can cause you to experience hurt and pain. But if you never acknowledge that you were ever wounded by certain things, you can hinder your healing. You should never become numb to what happened to cause you hurt and pain, be passive about it, or even try to tuck it away and forget about it. Don't ever be ashamed to say that you are hurting. Don't ever try to hide your pain. Be transparent. You are a human and you are not alone.

48

We all go through hurtful and painful periods in our lives, but it will not last forever.

When you do not address your hurt and pain, you neglect to receive the proper treatment that you need. The longer you harbor the hurt and pain, you make it easier for that hurt and pain to spill over into new friendships, relationships, etc. You may have heard someone say before that "Hurt people, hurt people." You see, your actions and responses in any given situation is a mere reflection of the hurt and pain that you have internalized. When you harbor hurt and pain long enough, you will find yourself paying a very dear price of just existing and not truly living. You will block your peace. You will block your joy. You can smile and laugh, but people will be able to see the hurt and pain behind your smile. You can make yourself appear to be happy by putting a fake smile on your face. But when you are genuinely happy for real, it will show, even if you do not smile.

As I shared in my story at the beginning of this book, up to July 14, 2019, I can honestly say that I had only existed without allowing myself to genuinely feel real joy. I knew pain all too well. I had to be healed and it had to start with me. I had to point the finger at myself and deal with myself. I had to be honest with myself. I had to start blaming myself. I had to forgive. I had to do what was needed to become a better version of myself.

Again, your healing starts with you, too. After you are honest with yourself, you need to be honest with God. When you tell Him the truth, He can help you. He already knows what you are dealing with. He already knows you are hurting. He already knows you are full of pain. He just wants to hear you say it. He wants you to confess it honestly out of your mouth. Ask God, right now, to make you whole, and mean it. Be willing to do what is required of you and what He instructs you to do to begin your healing. It will not magically happen. It is an intentional process daily; you have to be intentional about every detail of your life. If you want a happy and fulfilling life, it all starts with you doing something. If you want to be free, it all starts with you doing something. If you want to be healed, it all starts with you doing something.

John Chapter 5:5-9 KJV says the following: "*And a certain man was there, which had an infirmity thirty and eight years. When Jesus saw him lie, and knew that he had been now a long time in that case, he saith unto him, Wilt thou be made whole? The impotent man answered him, Sir, I have no man, when the water is troubled, to put me into the pool: but while I am coming, another steppeth down before me. Jesus saith unto him, Rise, take up thy bed, and walk. And immediately the man was made whole, and took up his bed, and walked: and on the same day was the sabbath.*" The key thing about this story is that this man was required to do something to secure his healing. It all started with him. He had to "rise, and then take up his bed and walk." I encourage you to do what is required of you to secure your healing.

QUETIA'S NUGGETS

❖ You have to make a decision to want to be healed, and then take action.

❖ If you want to be free, happy, healthy, and whole, you have work to do. It is not magic. It is intentional. You have to want it to get it.

❖ You need to heal properly so that you can be elevated and walk in your purpose.

❖ If you desire to be in a relationship, sometimes you have to master being by yourself first. It may hurt to be alone, but it is necessary for God to heal you and send you the right person that will love and show you unconditional love, with words and actions. I realize that no one is perfect, but if you allow someone in your life that does not reciprocate, it can only hurt you. You can become a "casualty of war" by letting someone into your personal space that should not be there.

CHAPTER SIX
LOVE YOURSELF AND OTHERS

"Beloved, if God so loved us, we ought also to love one another."
1 John 4:11 KJV

"To fall in love with yourself is the first secret to happiness."
-Robert Morley

"In the end nothing we do or say in this lifetime will matter as much as the way we have loved one another."
-Daphne Rose Kingma

The Merriam-Webster Dictionary defines love as "strong affection for another arising out of kinship or personal ties."

I want to share what love is from a godly perspective. In 1 Corinthians 13:4-8 NLT, we will find that "Love is patient and kind. Love is not jealous or boastful or proud or rude. It does not demand its own way. It is not irritable, and it keeps no record of being wronged. It does not rejoice about injustice but rejoices whenever the truth wins out. Love never gives up, never loses faith, is always hopeful, and endures through every circumstance. Prophecy and speaking in unknown languages and special knowledge will become useless. But love will last forever!"

The first thing each of us must learn to do is master loving ourselves. If you struggle with loving yourself, you will not be able to properly love others in your family, your friendships, or your relationship, if you are currently in one. You will blame and fault others for what you are lacking or perceive as lack. You will lead a life of searching for love, affection, and attention from the wrong people. You will only hurt yourself in the process and find yourself accepting less than what you really deserve when you search for love in the wrong people. Searching for steadfast, unconditional love in the wrong people will kill you internally. You will find yourself walking around for years with a broken heart and no one to fulfill your expectations. You cannot allow people in your life who cannot give you what you are expecting, and you should not expect to be in someone's life if you are not able to give what they are expecting: love. You see, when you learn to accept and love yourself, you will learn to genuinely love others.

QUETIA'S NUGGETS

❖ Love God first. Love yourself next. Love everyone else next. In that order.

❖ The best gift you can give a person is love.

❖ Begin to speak life into yourself, and then speak life into others. Believe what God said about you first. There are plenty of people smiling on the outside, but they do not like themselves on the inside. Beauty starts within, and so does love.

❖ You should thank God for creating you. Don't ever put yourself down. You are His creation and He loves every part of you. He wants you to love every part of yourself, too.

❖ Start showing yourself love by accepting yourself, including your shape, size, the color of your skin, and more. Look in the mirror every single day and say something positive and good about yourself. You can also start doing nice things for yourself. This is a part of loving who you are.

❖ Make sure you love others with the love of God.

❖ Never neglect yourself; that is not love.

❖ If you don't love yourself, there is just no way that you can properly love someone else.

❖ Don't hate anyone. Rather, love everyone, even those who may not reciprocate in any of your friendships or your relationship.

CHAPTER SEVEN
HOLD YOURSELF ACCOUNTABLE

"For we must all appear before the judgment seat of Christ; that every one may receive the things done in his body, according to that he hath done, whether it be good or bad."
2 Corinthians 5:10

"Personal accountability requires mindfulness, acceptance, honesty, and courage."
-Shelby Martin

The Merriam-Webster Dictionary defines "accountable" as "subject to giving an account: answerable."

There are so many people who lack accountability. At one point in my life, I was one of them. I had to deal with myself and God had to deal with me. As I shared before, I used to blame others for some of the things I did, but I had to come to a place in my life where I took ownership for my part. How could any of us expect to grow beyond where we are if we are always blaming other people for what we do or don't do? How could any of us even feel comfortable always shifting the blame?

It is necessary and right to hold yourself accountable for your actions. It is never okay to justify your wrongdoings. If you do something that is not right, then own what you did, because you are in control of how you think, act, and react to every situation you encounter. As I shared before, your decisions and choices, good or bad, are yours and yours alone. I have made some good and bad decisions, and I had to deal with the consequences of the bad ones.

Accepting responsibility for your actions shows a level of maturity. It shows courage and strength. People will respect and appreciate you more when they know that you are a person who is accountable. Some of them would even want to have you as their friend. Speaking of friends, each of us needs a friend who is going to hold us accountable. We need a friend who is going to tell us when we are wrong, even when it hurts. We need a friend who is going to encourage us to do what is morally right in any given situation. We need a friend who can sharpen us. The Bible tells us in Proverbs 27:17 NLT, "As iron sharpens iron, so a friend sharpens a friend."

QUETIA'S NUGGETS

❖ You must hold yourself accountable at all times. You can quickly check yourself when you feel like you want to blame someone else for your actions.

❖ Don't ever commit to doing something and not follow through with it, and then turn around and blame someone else for not doing what you committed to do.

❖ There comes a time where you have to look at yourself in the mirror and say, "It's me that I need to point the finger at, not other people"

❖ Take ownership for what you have allowed.

❖ It is your life. Begin to own it. Begin to own you, all of you.

CHAPTER EIGHT
RENEW YOUR MIND

"Do not conform to the pattern of this world, but be transformed by the renewing of your mind. Then you will be able to test and approve what God's will is—his good, pleasing and perfect will."
Romans 12:2 NIV

"We can't solve problems by using the same kind of thinking we used when we created them."
-Albert Einstein

The Merriam-Webster Dictionary defines "renew" as "to become new or as new; to make new spiritually." Philippians 2:5 KJV tells us to "Let this mind be in you, which was also in Christ Jesus."

You ought to make every effort to renew your mind daily. You need to make sure that your thoughts are positive, pure, and holy. When any of us have these kinds of thoughts, we benefit greatly.

I am certain that at some point you have had negative and bad thoughts and imaginations, but it is very important to "cast down those imaginations and bring into captivity those thoughts" whenever they come into your mind. (2 Corinthians 10:5). You are not alone. I have had bad thoughts before, and I have had to do this very thing.

I have had thoughts of my past, too. I have learned that the thoughts of your past can remain in your mind, influence your decisions, and hinder you from moving forward. Has anyone ever hurt you and caused you pain and you still think about how you were treated? Don't you know that the devil will use those negative thoughts of your past to torment you, make you blame others for what happened (even it if wasn't your fault), block your blessings, and more? God does not want that for you. He does not want you to entertain the thoughts of your past. He wants to replace those negative thoughts of your past with positive, pure, and holy thoughts.

I thank God for renewing my mind and for allowing me to see the error of my ways when my thoughts were not in alignment with the good. I know that He will do the same for you. Now my mind and thoughts are sending positive energy into my life. I have been intentionally directing my thoughts towards good and positive things, not negative things that can easily cause me to error in my ways. I encourage you to be intentional about directing your thoughts towards good and positive things, too. Be intentional daily.

QUETIA'S NUGGETS

❖ It is necessary to take some time to unwind and give God your full attention so that He can cleanse your mind from impure thoughts, negative thoughts, evil thoughts, etc. Be still. Be quiet and listen to Him.

❖ Set your affection on things above, not on things on the earth. Colossians 3:2 KJV.

❖ For to be carnally minded is death, but to be spiritually minded is life and peace. Romans 8:6 KJV.

❖ Create in me a clean heart, O God, and renew a right spirit within me. Psalm 51:10 KJV.

❖ Be careful for nothing; but in everything by prayer and supplication with thanksgiving let your requests be made known unto God. And the peace of God which passeth all understanding, shall keep your hearts and minds through Christ Jesus. Philippians 4:6-7 KJV.

DECLARATION

I encourage you to say this declaration every day, and let it get deep down in your spirit.

Today is the day that I love me right where I am. I love everything about me. I embrace all of my strengths, weaknesses, my successes, and my failures. I take full responsibility for me and my actions. Everything that I have done and everything I have gone through has been because of me and my decisions. I blame no one else for me.

Today, I take a stand for me. This is a very liberating day, a day of freedom. I no longer care what anyone thinks about me. I will look how I want to look and dress how I want to dress. I will be what size I want to be and I will love every inch of me. If there is anything about me that I don't like, I, along with God's help, am responsible for the change I need. I am me. I am _____ (insert your name). I am a victor and not a victim.

Today, I put God first. I know that He will never leave me or forsake me. It is time for isolation, a time for me to spend time with God. I must understand that everyone is not going to like me, no matter how good I am to them. I must realize that I cannot please everybody. I must realize that I have to love and care about me before I can love and care for someone else. I am not in a competition with anyone and I will not allow people to make me feel that I am. I am me and I am unique. God made only one of me. I will be 100% me. I am not faking or auditioning for any roles. I will laugh

65

when people try to talk about me, because it only lets me know that they are thinking of me. From now on, I am just going to be me and have no apologies for being who God created me to be.

Thank You, Jesus!

"Signed, Sealed, Delivered"

_____

(Sign your name here and date)

ABOUT THE AUTHOR

Laquetia Yvonne Mercer is a minister, author, certified life coach, motivational speaker, and an Eastern Star. She lives in Birmingham, Alabama. She was raised by her grandparents who nurtured her and introduced her to Jesus Christ. They faithfully took her to church every Sunday. She fostered a love for the Lord as a young girl. She is the mother of three children, two boys and one girl, and takes every opportunity to share knowledge with her children and others as well.

Laquetia is a gifted and powerful woman of God. She has allowed God to turn her pain into power and she believes that He has bestowed many gifts and talents upon her. She is even more confident in knowing that her purpose is far greater than the pain she encountered.

CONTACT THE AUTHOR

If you would like to contact the author, you may reach out to her by email at laquetianewstartmercer@gmail.com.

THE BLAME GAME IS OVER

JOURNAL

I encourage you to use this section of the book as your personal journal. You may answer the journal questions and make notes, etc.

JOURNAL QUESTIONS FOR CHAPTER ONE
(SELF-EVALUATION)

"The truth will set you free, but first it will make you miserable." –James A. Garfield

1. Are you ready to be honest and take responsibility for your life?
2. Are you ready to be honest with yourself about you?
3. Are you ready to be honest with God about you and confess it out of your mouth so that he can help you along with you helping yourself?
4. What was your part in it?
5. Are you ready to do a self-evaluation?
6. Do you feel that it is necessary for you to do a self-evaluation daily?
7. Do you ever consider your ways?
8. Do you want to change some or all of your ways?
9. What areas would you like to work on now?

THE BLAME GAME IS OVER

_____

_____

_____

_____

_____

_____

_____

_____

_____

_____

_____

_____

_____

_____

_____

_____

_____

_____

_____

_____

_____

_____

_____

_____

JOURNAL QUESTIONS FOR CHAPTER TWO
(ADMIT AND CONFESS)

Free yourself by admitting and confessing.

1. Are you ready to admit and confess your faults, shortcomings, etc.?
2. Are you a person that will lie and blame others for something you do wrong or are you the one who is often lied on and blamed for something others do wrong?
3. Who have you been blaming and why have you been blaming them?
4. What are your flaws and bad habits?
5. What decisions have you made that have caused adverse effects in your life?
6. To stop blaming is a decision. Are you ready to stop blaming?
7. Do you want to be free in your mind, body, and soul?
8. Will you commit to making better decisions intentionally daily?

_____

_____

_____

_____

_____

_____

_____

_____

_____

_____

_____

_____

_____

_____

_____

_____

_____

_____

_____

_____

_____

_____

_____

_____

_____

_____

JOURNAL QUESTIONS FOR CHAPTER THREE
(REPENT)

God wants you to live your best life.

1. Do you understand how important it is to repent daily?
2. Will you stop making excuses?
3. Will you stop justifying your wrong and be honest with yourself and God about it?
4. Will you disconnect from negative-minded people?
5. Do you honestly want to become a better person?

JOURNAL QUESTIONS FOR CHAPTER FOUR
(FORGIVE YOURSELF AND OTHERS)

Forgiveness is a decision and it frees you.

1. Will you make a solid decision to forgive?
2. Who do you need to forgive so that you can be forgiven?
3. Will you forgive yourself?

_____

_____

_____

_____

_____

_____

_____

_____

_____

_____

_____

_____

_____

_____

_____

_____

_____

_____

_____

_____

_____

_____

_____

JOURNAL QUESTIONS FOR CHAPTER FIVE
(BE HEALED)

Healing is a decision. It begins with you.

1. Do you want to be healed?
2. What steps will you take towards your healing? Write down all the steps that you can think of at this moment. Be sure to make a conscious effort to take action.
3. Do you need a counselor, therapist, life coach, pastor, or support group? If so, are you willing to invest in yourself and get the help you need? Remember, it is not magic. You have to be intentional daily. You have work to do in order to be healed.

JOURNAL QUESTIONS FOR CHAPTER SIX
(LOVE YOURSELF AND OTHERS)

Matthew 22:36-40 KJV
Master, which is the great commandment in the law? Jesus said unto him, Thou shalt love the Lord thy God with all thy heart, and with all thy soul, and with all thy mind. This is the first and great commandment. And the second is like unto it, thou shalt love thy neighbour as thyself. On these two commandments hang all the law and the prophets.

1. Do you love God?
2. Do you love yourself?
3. Do you love others?
4. In what ways will you begin to show love in your everyday life so that you can walk in your purpose? God has a purpose for you and your life.

JOURNAL QUESTIONS FOR CHAPTER SEVEN
(HOLD YOURSELF ACCOUNTABLE)

One of the best things you can do is hold yourself accountable.

1. Will you take ownership for the things and people that you have allowed in your life?
2. Will you assume responsibility for your actions?
3. Will you work daily towards becoming the best version of yourself? What steps will you take?
4. What area of your life will you work on first?
5. Do you have a friend that will hold you accountable? If not, you can find a pastor, life coach, or pray that God sends you that friend who will truly and honestly hold you accountable.

JOURNAL QUESTIONS FOR CHAPTER EIGHT
(RENEWING YOUR MIND)

Renewing your mind is a decision. It is an intentional, conscious decision every minute of the day. It takes action.

1. What time of day will you spend time with God, talk to him, pray to him, listen to him, worship and praise him, and read your bible?
2. Will you intentionally begin to change the negative into positive in every area of your life?
3. Will you change the company you keep if they are not good for you and your new life? "You are who you are by virtue of the company you keep." –T.B. Joshua
4. What type of positive things will you listen to?
5. What type of positive books will you read?
6. What type of positive music and TV shows will you watch?

OTHER JOURNAL QUESTIONS

1. My perspective about my pain and or grief has to change wholeheartedly so that I can move forward into what God has for me. Change your mind and change your life. What changes will you make?
2. Did I offend myself by wanting more out of others than they wanted for themselves? Take time to truthfully answer this question.
3. How do you respond and or perceive what you have been through?
4. How can you use what you have been through to help others?
5. What is your plan for becoming a better person? What area of your life are you going to begin working towards becoming a better you?
6. Are you ready for a new beginning? What will be your first step towards your new beginning?

www.ingramcontent.com/pod-product-compliance
Lightning Source LLC
Chambersburg PA
CBHW071150090426
42736CB00012B/2289